Raw Vegan Cuisine & Fermented Foods

Gourmet & Cultured Living Raw Food Recipes

By: Kevin Kerr

2 Raw Vegan Cuisine & Fermented Foods

In no way is it legal to reproduce, duplicate, or transmit any part of this document in either electronic means or in printed format. Recording of this publication is strictly prohibited and any storage of this document is not allowed unless with written permission from the publisher.

Copyright © 2015 by Kevin Kerr

All rights reserved.

Table of Contents

Introduction
Rawghetti (p.8)
Raw Burgers (p.9)
Raw Sweet Onion Potato Bread (p.10)
Rawza (p.11)
Sauerkraut (p.13)
Coconut Yogurt (p.14)
Kombucha (p.15)
Kimchi (p.16)
Raw Lasagna (p.17)
Alfredo Pasta (p.20)
Raw Chocolate (p.21)
Carrot Cake (p.22)
Raw Apple Apricot Cobbler (p.24)
Watermelon Cake (p.25)
Vanilla Cheesecake (p.26)
Cinnamon Cake (p.27)
Coconut Cream Pie (p.29)
Raw Pumpkin Pie (p.31)
Maple Ice Cream (p.33)
Brownies and Caramel Sauce (p.34)
Raw Chocolate Nut Butter Cookies (p.35)
Raw Fig Cookies(p.36)
Chocolate Chip Cookies (p.37)
Oatmeal Raisin Cookies (p.38)
Chocolate Macadamia Nut Cookies (p.40)
Gingerbread Cookies (p.41)
Chocolate Pumpkin Brownies (p.42)

5 Raw Vegan Cuisine & Fermented Foods

Oreos (p.43)
Chocolate Truffles (p.45)
Almond Butter Cups (p.46)

Introduction

Raw vegan gourmet and fermented recipes are the most delicious and nutritious recipes on the planet. Aside from tasting better, being better for your body, and being cruelty-free; uncooked vegan food takes less prep time. I personally love these recipes and use one or more every day. Raw meals are so beneficial for the human body because they practically digest themselves. Raw food is anything that isn't heated over 118 degrees so that the precious enzymes aren't destroyed. In order for food to digest it must be broken down by enzymes. Science has recently discovered that our bodies can only produce so many enzymes in this lifetime which is the number one reason to eat as much raw food as you enjoy.

There are three ways that digestive enzymes are produced which are by plants, by our body, and by the 400,000 to 800,000 bacteria that live in our gut. Studies have conclusively shown that people who are overweight have less gut bacteria so the best way to replenish them by making fermented foods and repopulate your already existent colony by eating fruit! Fermenting fruits, vegetables, nuts, seeds, mushrooms and herbs can be as simple as cutting or blending them up and putting them in mason jars with water and salt. Let the jars sit out for several days or longer depending on the taste you enjoy. Be sure to try them periodically and when you find a taste you like put the jars in the refrigerator where they will remain good for many months. You can add raw apple cider vinegar or a capsule of probiotics to speed up the fermentation process. Superfoods can also be added for more nutritional value!

Rawghetti

- 1 to 3 zucchini depending on the size
- 1 ¼ cup grape tomatoes
- ½ yellow bell pepper
- 2 cloves garlic
- 2 tablespoons chopped red onion
- 5 to 7 fresh basil leaves
- 4 tablespoons olive oil
- sea salt to taste

Prepare zucchini by cutting of both ends. Using a vegetable peeler (or preferably a spiralizer) turn your zucchini into spaghetti strips (leave the skin on if organic). In a big bowl stir in zucchini with 1 tablespoon of olive oil and a pinch or two of sea salt. Blend the remaining ingredients in a blender until a chunky even consistency is reached. If your sauce is too thick for your liking I recommend adding more grape tomatoes or a ¼ cup water. Before enjoying this delicious meal, sprinkle with sea salt, nutritional yeast, and hemp seeds!

Serves: 1 to 3.

Raw Burgers

- 8 pieces romaine lettuce
- 1 avocado
- ¾ cup brazil nuts
- 4 slices red onion
- 2 medium-sized heirloom tomatoes
- ½ cucumber
- 2 teaspoons pink Himalayan salt
- 15-20 halved grape tomatoes

Take 1 pieces of lettuce for each side of your "bun". Fold both pieces in half and press them firm against a table so that the lettuce breaks to form an even surface. You will be making 4 sandwiches. Using a food processor or high speed blender, mix the avocado, brazil nuts, and salt. Evenly disperse the mixture onto the four slices, and place the grape tomatoes on top. Slice and add your desired amount of toppings. Enjoy!

Serves: 2.

Raw Sweet Onion Potato Bread

- 2 pounds of peeled sweet onions
- 3 peeled red potatoes
- 1 cup chia seeds
- 1 cup pumpkin seeds
- ⅓ cup olive oil
- 1 teaspoon sea salt

First start by blending or milling the pumpkin seeds and chia seeds. Put in a bowl with the olive oil and salt. Use a food processor for the onions and potatoes, or cut them into pea-sized pieces with a knife. Mix all the ingredients together. It should form a thick paste-like substance, if not simply add a tablespoon of water or olive oil. Using a dehydrator, heat between 100 to 105 degrees for 6 to 9 hours. This recipes typically yields between 3 to 4 trays of deliciousness. Flip your sheets of bread half way to achieve an even consistency. ENJOY!

Serves: 5 to 7.

Rawza

In order to create raw pizza, it's necessary to first make the crusts. They can be stored in the freezer for several days in an airtight bag or container.

- 1 ½ cup almonds
- ½ cup brazil nuts
- 1 cup chia seeds
- 1 cup water
- 2 tablespoons olive oil
- 1 tablespoon dried basil
- 1 tablespoon dried rosemary
- 1 tablespoon dried oregano
- 1 teaspoon of pink Himalayan salt

First, mill all the nuts and seeds in a food processor or high powered blender until they are a flour-like substance. Mix the rest of the ingredients in a bowl together with your ground up nuts and seeds. Shape your crusts on a dehydrator tray coated with coconut oil, but don't make them more than ⅜ inch thick. Dehydrate at 105 degrees for 9 to 13 hours. Now it's time to make the sauce!

- 3 cups tomatoes
- 10 dried tomatoes (soak overnight)
- 2 dried and pitted dates (soak overnight)
- ¼ inch slice of red onion
- ½ cup olive oil
- 2 tablespoons dried parsley

- 4 cloves garlic
- ¼ teaspoon cayenne (optional)
- 1 teaspoon pink Himalayan salt

Mix to an even consistency using a food processor or high speed blender, then spread on your crusts. Top with nutritional yeast and your favorite pizza toppings! Eat right away or heat in the dehydrator!

Serves: 2 to 3.

Sauerkraut

- Cut one head of your favorite cabbage up into thin edible strips (about 2 lbs.)
- Rub 2 tablespoons of salt into the cut up vegetable
- Put salted cabbage into a jar with a tablespoon of caraway seeds
- Next put another jar, upside down, into the first jar with a cheese cloth over everything so that nothing enters the batch
- Weigh the jar down so that pressure keeps the cabbage together
- Within an hour the cabbage should be submerged in its own juice
- Taste test every few days until it is ready to go in the fridge

Enjoy!

Coconut Yogurt

- cut the top off of a coconut or and drain into your blender
- scrape the meat into the blender
- add 2 to 3 cups of your favorite soaked nuts or seeds
- add a live strain of probiotics
- blend and put in a mason jar and leave the lid slightly open
- let it set out for about two hours then and then put it in the fridge
- Let sit in the fridge for at least 24 hours to allow the bacteria to colonize
- consume within a week
- Optional add ins: your favorite fruits or superfood powders

Add to smoothies, dressings, or indulge on it's own.

Enjoy!

Kombucha

- Things you will need include: a gallon glass jug, cheese cloth, a rubber band, a Kombucha starter culture, 10 bags of black tea, a wooden spoon, a pot to boil water, and a cup of raw organic cane sugar
- Start by boiling water
- Let tea sit and brew for twenty minutes
- Stir in sugar
- Let tea cool and put in culture
- Cover with cheese cloth and wrap with rubber band
- Let it sit out for several weeks or until taste is satisfactory
- Refrigeration stops the fermentation process

You can also add your favorite fruit to give your Kombucha additional flavors or experiment using different teas!

Enjoy!

Kimchi

- 2 lbs. cabbage
- 1 medium apple
- 1 small chopped red onion
- 2 cloves garlic
- 1 tbsp. cayenne powder
- ¼ cup pink Himalayan Salt
- 6 cups water

Directions: Cut cabbage up into appropriate bite-sized pieces. Put it in a bowl after this is completed with the salt and 2 cups of warm water. Mix it well with your hands and let it sit for at least two hours, up to 12. While this is soaking blend the rest of the ingredients including the four cups of reserved water. Drain off the cabbage brine into another bowl or cup. Add blended mixture to cabbage with one cup of brine from the drained liquid. Mix together well. Add to mason jars. Add more brine if necessary so that all cabbage is covered. Cover your jars with cheese cloth for one to four days. Try it periodically until you find the desired taste you enjoy. Once you do, seal the mixtures and put them in the refrigerator. Consume within two months.

Enjoy!

Raw Lasagna

Cheese Sauce:
- 2 cups soaked macadamia nuts
- 1 cup soaked cashews
- 2 tbsps. lemon
- 2 tbsps. nutritional yeast
- 1 orange bell pepper
- 2 tbsps. fresh parsley
- 1 tbsp. fresh thyme
- ½ tsp. sea salt
- ½ cup water

Blend and set said or put in refrigerator.

Meat Layer:
- ½ cup soaked walnuts
- 1 cup soaked sun dried tomatoes
- 2 tsps. oregano
- 2 tsps. sage
- ½ tsp. sea salt
- 1 tbsp. pine nuts

Process ingredients leaving it slightly chunky.

Tomato Sauce:
- 1 ½ cups soaked sun dried tomatoes
- 2 pitted dried medjool dates
- 2 cloves garlic
- 1 large heirloom tomato
- 1 tbsp. oregano
- 2 tbsps. olive oil
- 2 tbsps. lemon juice

Blend until smooth.

Pesto:
- 2 cups basil leaves
- ¾ cup pine nuts
- 3 tbsps. hemp seed oil
- 1 clove garlic
- 1 tbsp. lemon juice
- ½ tsp. salt

Process ingredients leaving it slightly chunky.

Spinach Layer:
- 6 cups torn layer
- 5 tbsps. oregano
- 1 tsp. olive oil
- ¼ tsp. sea salt

Mix ingredients in a bowl and let sit for 1 hour.

Pasta Layer:
- 5 zucchinis cut lengthwise into thin strips
- ½ tsp olive oil
- pinch of black or cayenne pepper
- 5 leaves of chopped basil

Marinate for 10 minutes.

Assembly:
Line the bottom of your pan or glass with half of the zucchini strips. Then add a layer of half of the meat layer, all the cheese, all the tomato sauce, and followed by all of the pesto.

Add the rest of the meat layer, followed by all of the spinach layer, and top it off with the rest of the zucchini pasta. Although it is not necessary you can refrigerate or dehydrate your raw lasagne to firm it up a little bit which will make it easier to cut. This recipes serves 8 to 10.

Enjoy!

Alfredo Pasta

Sauce:
- 2 cups chopped parsnips
- 2 cloves garlic
- 3 fresh sage leaves
- 1 tsp. thyme
- 1 tbsp. cashew butter
- ½ cup nutritional yeast
- ¼ cup walnut butter
- 1 cup water
- sea salt to taste

Blend until smooth!

For the pasta spiralize 6 cups of parsnips or zucchini. Add 2 cups of sliced crimini mushrooms, ½ small chopped red onion and 2 tbsps. chopped fresh sage.

Serves: 1 or 2.

Enjoy!

Raw Chocolate
- 4 ounces raw organic cacao butter
- 3 ounces raw organic coconut oil
- 4 to 6 tbsps. raw organic cacao powder
- 2 tsps. cinnamon
- Coconut sugar, lo han guo, goji berry, lucuma, maple syrup, cane sugar, stevia, schizandra berry, or yacon. You decide! I recommend lo han guo, stevia, or maple syrup for chocolate.

First, melt the cacao butter and coconut oil in your double-broiler system at the lowest temperature possible to save nutrients. Next, stir in the cacao powder, cinnamon and sweetener until you get a consistent "chocolate syrup". Pour into a plate or silicone molds and put into the refrigerator until it hardens up. It usually only takes an hour or less. Break into pieces or free from molds and enjoy! :)

Optional: If you want to get creative you can add dried fruits before you refrigerate such as dates, goji berries or mulberries. If you really want to make things interesting and healthy try adding nuts or seeds, nut butters, or superfood powders!

Carrot Cake

Macadamia Nut Frosting:
- 1 ½ cups macadamia nuts
- juice from 1 lemon
- 2 tbsps. liquefied coconut oil
- 2 tbsps. coconut sugar
- 1 tsp. vanilla powder
- 1 tbsp. water

Carrot Cake:
- 3 large carrots, peeled and chopped into small chunks or pulp from 6 large carrots that were juiced
- 1 ½ cups oats
- 2 cups pitted dates
- ½ cup dried coconut powder
- 1 tsp. cinnamon
- ½ tsp. nutmeg

Frosting:

Blend all ingredients in your high speed blender until smooth, adding water as needed. Put in the fridge for at least an hour before using.

Cake:

Process the oats into flour in your food processor then add the rest of the ingredients in and process until it begins to stick together. Put the mixture into a bowl to form it into your cake or simply construct it into your desired shape then put in the freezer until it's solid. Then simply frost your cake and you officially have the healthiest and most delicious carrot cake in the world! Enjoy!

Serves: 3 to 4.

Raw Apple Apricot Cobbler

- 8 peeled and cored apples
- 4 sliced and quartered apricots
- ¼ cup organic maple syrup
- 3 tbsps. liquefied coconut oil
- 1 tsp. cinnamon
- ¼ tsp. sea salt

Mix all the ingredients except for the apricots in a blender or food processor until an even consistency is reached, then mix in the chunks of apricots but keep them whole. This will be used as the filling to this delicious dessert. Now it's time to make the shell and topping.

- 1 cup walnuts
- 1 cup dried pitted dates
- 3 tbsps. coconut oil
- 2 tsps. cinnamon
- 1 ½ tsps. vanilla extract or 1 vanilla bean

Mix the ingredients in a food processor or blender until an even chunky consistency is reached. Pour into a pyrex pie crust but save enough for the topping. Top and serve! Fit for ten people. If you desire it warm you can heat at the lowest temperature possible in your oven or dehydrator for 20 minutes to several hours.

Serves: 4 to 6.

Watermelon Cake

- 1 watermelon
- 1 cup soaked hemp seeds
- 1 cup soaked cashews
- ½ cup coconut water
- 1 juiced lemon
- 2 vanilla beans
- 3 tbsps. raw honey
- ½ cup soaked almonds

Start by peeling the watermelon and shaping it to your desired size of cake(s). (Cup cakes are also possible.) Next, blend or process the rest of the ingredients until smooth. Cover the entire watermelon. Process the almonds and stick them to the sides of your cake. Top with your favorite fruits and refrigerate for an hour!

Serves: 3 to 6.

Vanilla Cheesecake

Crust:

- 1 cup pitted medjool dates
- 2 cups raw almonds

Surround the inside of a cake pan with wax paper or plastic wrap. Pulse dates and nuts together in food processor until you get an even consistency. Form and press mixture into the bottom of the pan. Put in fridge for at least an hour before putting the cake together.

Cheesecake:

- 3 cups soaked raw cashews
- ¾ cup lemon juice
- ⅔ cup maple syrup
- ¾ cup liquefied coconut oil
- ½ tsp. sea salt
- 1 tsp. vanilla extract
- 1 vanilla bean

Blend all ingredients, except coconut oil, together until smooth and creamy. Add coconut oil and make sure it blends completely. Pour onto crust in cake pan and set in the fridge for at least two hours. Take out of cake pan holding onto the wax paper or plastic wrap and put it on a plate.

Slice and enjoy!

Serves: 2 to 6.

Cinnamon Cake

Dough:

- 1 cup pecans
- ½ cup ground flax seeds
- ¼ cup maple syrup
- 3 tbsps. raw buckwheat flour
- 5 pitted dates

Filling:

- ½ cup pitted medjool dates
- ¼ cup water
- 2 tbsps. cinnamon
- 1 tbsp./ liquefied coconut oil
- ¼ tsp. sea salt
- 4 pitted medjool dates
- 2 tbsps. chopped hazelnuts

Icing:

- 1 cup cashews
- ¼ cup coconut oil
- 4 tbsps. fresh squeezed lemon juice
- 1 tbsp. maple syrup

Directions

- Mix all of the dough ingredients in a food processor until it starts sticking together until it forms a dough. Set aside.
- Mix all of the filling ingredients in a food processor or a blender until well blended.
- In a medium sized spring form pan or form your cake to the desired shape you want with your hands.
- Put in the freezer for about an hour to make it easier to apply icing.
- Mix all of the icing ingredients in a food processor or blend together until desired consistency is reached.
- Ice the cake!
- Top with cinnamon and your favorite chopped nuts.

Serves: 4 to 7.

Enjoy!

Coconut Cream Pie

Crust:
- 1 ½ cups nuts
- 1 ½ cups pitted medjool dates
- pinch of sea salt

Chocolate Cream:
- 2 avocados
- ⅓ cup maple syrup
- ½ tsp. cinnamon
- ¼ cup raw cacao powder
- 2 tbsps. mesquite powder
- 2 tbsps. liquefied coconut oil
- pinch of sea salt

Whipped Cream:
- 1 ½ cups of coconut milk
- 3 tbsps. raw coconut sugar
- 1 vanilla bean

Crust:

Pulse nuts in food processor until they're the size of crumbs. Add dates and pulse until it lumps together. Feel free to add cinnamon, salt, vanilla or more sweeteners here. Press into your favorite pie pan and stick in the fridge.

Chocolate Cream:

Blend or process all ingredients until silky smooth. Now slice 3-4 bananas and put them on the bottom of the crust. Spoon on the chocolate cream and put on another player of banana slices. Set in the fridge again.

Right before serving, take out coconut milk from the fridge. Spoon off the thick fat from the top - you want this. Put the milk you spooned out into a mixing bowl with the sugar and beat until it turns into a cream! Spoon over your pie and enjoy!

Serves: 3 to 4.

Raw Pumpkin Pie

Crust:

- 1 cup cashews
- 1 cup almonds
- ¼ cup pitted medjool dates
- 1 cup dates
- ⅛ tsp. sea salt

Pumpkin Filling:

- 1 cubed pie pumpkin without the seeds
- 1 cup dates
- 4 tbsps. liquefied coconut oil
- ⅓ cup maple syrup
- 3 tbsps. pumpkin pie spices (cinnamon, nutmeg, ginger and cloves)

Crust:

Process the nuts in your food processor until they are like a rough flour. add the dates, raisins and salt. Pulse until it all sticks together in a lump. Press into the bottom of a pie dish and refrigerate.

Pie Filling:

Process the pumpkin cubes until they can't get any smaller in your food processor. Add in the other ingredients and process until it can't get any smoother. Transfer the filling to your high speed blender and blend on the highest setting until an even consistency is reached. Spread the filling onto your pie crust and let it set in the fridge for a few hours.

Serves: 3 to 6.

Maple Ice Cream

- 2 frozen bananas
- 1-2 tbsps. maple syrup
- 1/4 cup walnuts
- dash of cinnamon, to taste
- dash of nutmeg, to taste

Blend the bananas and maple syrup until smooth, in a food processor.

Add in the walnuts and spices, to taste. Blend and enjoy!

Serves: 1 or 2.

Brownies and Caramel Sauce

- 1 cup raw cacao powder
- 1 cup walnuts
- 1 cup pecans
- ¼ cup hemp seeds
- ¾ cup dried pitted dates
- 1 tsp. maple syrup
- ¼ tsp. sea salt

Using a food processor or high speed blender, mill and mix the ingredients until a thick batter-like consistency is reached. Put your brownie mix into a container, or form into individual treats. They are delicious without the sauce, but mixing the following ingredients in a blender will provide you with the perfect raw caramel sauce!

- 1 tbsp. raw cacao powder
- 1 tsp. mesquite powder
- 1 tsp. lucuma powder
- 4 tsps. maple syrup
- 1 tsp. organic maple syrup
- 1 tsp. coconut oil

Blend well, top brownies, and enjoy! Serves: 3 to 6.

Raw Chocolate Nut Butter Cookies

- 1 cup of your favorite raw nuts or seeds
- ½ cup of your favorite raw nut or seed butter
- ½ cup dried pitted dates
- 2 tbsps. raw cacao nibs
- 2 tbsps. maple syrup
- 2 tbsps. coconut oil

Blend or process all the ingredients until a cookie dough consistency is reached. Form into your desired shapes and refrigerate for at least one hour. Next, place the following ingredients in a bowl and dip each cookie.

- 3 tbsps. liquefied coconut oil
- 3 tbsps. raw cacao powder
- 2 tbsps. maple syrup

Serves: 2 to 4.

Raw Fig Cookies

- 2 pound raw figs
- 1 cup hemp seeds
- ½ cup macadamia nuts
- 2 tbsps. maple syrup
- ¼ tsp. sea salt

First process or blend figs and set aside. Next, process or blend ½ cup hemp seeds, macadamia nuts, and salt. Add the rest of the hemp seeds, and mix together with a spoon. Form figs into desired shapes and cover with the milled nuts and seeds! ENJOY!

Serves: 4 to 10.

Chocolate Chip Cookies

- 1/2 cup raw organic walnuts
- 1/2 cup raw organic cashews
- 1 cup of your favorite variety of pitted dates
- 6 drops vanilla extract or ½ tsp. dried vanilla bean powder
- 4 oz of your favorite organic chocolate bar
- 1 tsp. maca powder

Blend or process all of the ingredients. A tbsp. of water may be necessary depending on how dry the dates are. This can be prevented by soaking them for 2 hours prior to making the recipe.

Form into cookies, Enjoy!

Makes about 5 to 7 servings.

Oatmeal Raisin Cookies

- 2 cups raw organic oats
- 1 cup raw pecans
- 1/2 cup firmly packed grated fresh apple (about 2 medium apples)
- 1 cup dried raisins
- 1/2 cup pitted dates
- 4 Tbsps. organic liquefied coconut oil
- 3 tbsps. coconut sugar
- 1 tsp. ground cinnamon
- 1/2 tsp. ground ginger
- 1 tsp. alcohol free vanilla extract
- 1 tbsp. freshly grated lemon zest
- pinch sea salt

Directions:

1. Add the pecans into a food processor fitted with the S blade, and a few times until roughly chopped. Empty them into a mixing bowl.
2. Place the oats in the food processor with the cinnamon, ginger, vanilla, sweetener, and sea salt and pulse a few times until well combined.
3. Add in the dates, apple, lemon zest, coconut oil and pulse again.
4. Transfer this mixture to a large bowl and fold through the remaining ingredients until a thick clustered "dough" forms.
5. Tweak the flavors to taste. You might want

more sweetener, cinnamon or lemon zest.
6. Form this dough into medium sized cookies and place on mesh dehydrator sheets.
7. Dehydrate cookies in your dehydrator at 100 degrees for 12 - 15 hours or more depending on your preference.
8. This recipe yields 12 medium-sized dense chewy cookies. Alternatively, you could make 24 smaller cookies.

Note: For those of you without a dehydrator, you can try making these oatmeal cookies in a conventional oven by preheating your oven to 300 F, placing the cookies in, closing the oven door, turning the oven off and allowing it to cool with the cookies inside. The cookies should have a nice chewy texture.

Chocolate Macadamia Nut Cookies

- 2 cups organic raw macadamia nuts
- ½ cup raw organic cacao powder
- 2 tbsps. liquefied organic coconut oil
- ½ cup organic raw agave or maple syrup
- 2 tsp organic vanilla extract
- ½ tsp sea salt

Directions:

1. Place the macadamia nuts in the food processor and pulse a few times until coarsely ground.
2. Now add in the cacao powder and pulse a few times until the consistency of bread crumbs.
3. Add in all of the other ingredients and pulse until well combined. The mixture should form a ball.
4. Take this ball and roll it out to about a 1/4 inch on parchment paper.
5. Now cut out even small circles. I used the top of a shot glass.
6. Place these circles on dehydrator sheets and slowly warm at 115 degrees for 48 hours.
7. Store in a sealed container in the fridge for about 3 weeks.

Serves: 5. Enjoy!

Gingerbread Cookies

- 2 cups of your favorite raw flour
- 1 ½ cups pitted dates
- ⅛ tsp. sea salt
- ½ tsp. vanilla powder
- 2 tbsps. fresh ginger
- 1 tsp. cinnamon
- 1 tsp. nutmeg
- 1 tbsp. molasses
- ¼ cup maple syrup
- 2 tbsps. liquefied coconut oil

Directions:

Place all the ingredients in a food processor or blender and mix until even consistency is reached. Form into cookies and enjoy!

Serves 4 to 8.

Chocolate Pumpkin Brownies

- 1 pie pumpkin
- 2 ½ lbs. pitted dates
- 3 ripe persimmons
- ½ raw cacao powder
- 1 tbsp. cinnamon
- 1 cup raw organic pecans
- 1 cup dried black mission figs
- 1 Tbs. pumpkin spices (nutmeg and clove)
- 1 thumb-sized chunk of ginger
- 1 small vanilla bean

Directions:

Add everything to your high speed blender and blend until even consistency is reached. Form into brownies and enjoy!

Serves 5 to 7.

Oreos

- ½ cup almonds
- ¼ cup ground flax or chia seeds
- ¼ cup raw cacao powder
- ¼ cup shredded coconut
- 1 tbsp. maple syrup
- 1 tsp. vanilla extract

For the stuffing:

- ¼ cup cashews
- 2 tbsps. shredded coconut
- 2 tbsps. liquefied coconut oil
- 1 tbsp. honey or maple syrup
- 1 tsp. vanilla extract

Directions:

Blend the almonds and flax meal in a food processor until the almonds are a powder.

Add in the cacao, shredded coconut, sweetener and vanilla. Blend until the dough starts to stick together. You may need to add a splash of water.

You can either roll the dough out into a cylinder and cut the cookies that way or roll out the mixture and use a cookie cutter. I opted for the latter and used the lid from a bottle that was the perfect size. Make sure to have an even number of oreo halves at the end!

Place them in a dehydrator overnight or if you

don't have one you can refrigerate.

Now it's time to do the filling! Blend up all of the ingredients in a food processor.

Sandwich the filling between the cookies and enjoy!

Serves: 4 to 6.

Chocolate Truffles

- 1 cup pitted dates
- ¼ cup hemp hearts for the recipe and a little extra for rolling truffles in
- 1 heaping tbsp. of cacao powder and a little extra for rolling truffles in

Directions:

Blend the dates, hemp hearts and cacao in a food processor until the mixture sticks together. If your dates are super moist, you could even do this by hand in a bowl if you don't have a food processor.

Roll the mixture into balls.

Roll the truffles in some cacao powder, hemp hearts, leave them plain or all of the above!

Enjoy!

Serves: 2 to 4.

Almond Butter Cups

- ¼ cup liquefied coconut oil
- ¼ cup raw organic cacao powder
- 1 tsp. maple syrup
- 2 tbsps. almond butter

Directions:

Mix cacao powder and sweetener of choice in with coconut oil in a small bowl.

Fill 6 little paper cupcake cups with about a tsp. of the chocolate in each.

Place in freezer for 5 minutes or until hardened.

Put a dollop of almond butter in each cup.

Cover with the remaining chocolate.

Freeze for another 5 minutes or until hardened.

Enjoy!

Serves: 3 to 4.

Made in United States
Orlando, FL
15 September 2023